TH€ €UROP€AN UNION! SHOULD W€ STAY OR SHOULD W€ GO?

Legal stuff:

THE AUTHOR AND PUBLISHER HAVE MADE THEIR BEST EFFORTS TO PRODUCE A HIGH QUALITY, INFORMATIVE AND HELPFUL VEHICLE. BUT THEY MAKE NO REPRESENTATION OR WARRANTIES OF ANY KIND WITH REGARD TO THE COMPLETENESS OR ACCURACY OF THE CONTENTS. THEY DO NOT ADVOCATE OR SUGGEST OR MAKE RECOMMENDATIONS OF ANY KIND AND ACCEPT NO LIABILITY OF ANY KIND FOR ANY LOSSES OR DAMAGES CAUSED OR ALLEGED TO BE CAUSED, DIRECTLY OR INDIRECTLY, FROM USING THE INFORMATION OR MATERIALS FOUND WITHIN

THE €UROP€AN UNION! SHOULD W€ STAY OR SHOULD W€ GO?

Did We Have Enough Information To Make Our Decision?

By

Ted Moss

A Book In The

Series Of Social Commentary

THE €UROP€AN UNION!
SHOULD W€ STAY OR SHOULD W€ GO?

All Rights Reserved © eam 2020

DEDICATION

This book is dedicated in the memory of Donna Lopez (26th February 1966 – 24th August 2020). After struggling with the pain and fears and then the hopes and promises, which turn out to be the cruel games that cancer plays, my very dear, intelligent friend and colleague succumbed to the filthy disease at the age of 54 years.

PREFACE

Back in early 2016 David Cameron's Tory government spent £9 million sending leaflets to every house in the UK offering all eligible persons a vote in the upcoming United Kingdom European Union membership referendum, better known as the *Brexit* referendum or the EU exit referendum.

The actual vote took place on June the 23rd and the electorate and Sovereign people of Great Britain and those living in her overseas territories, for example Gibraltar were asked to decide whether the United Kingdom should remain a member of the (EU) European Union, or whether the United Kingdom should leave the European Union.

That was it, it could not have been any simpler or clearer to understand and for Government to act on. *Should we stay in the European Union or should we leave the European Union?* And as we know the people voted to leave.

In his resignation speech (or with hindsight, perhaps it was more of an escape speech) the Prime Minister, David (call me Dave) Cameron stated that the British people had spoken and *"their will must be respected"*.

However, things have not gone as smoothly as good ol' Dave had ordered.

The Sovereign people of Great Britain and those living in her overseas territories might have said: come out of the European Union... Now! But that did not happen, as some members of the government, some in opposition and some from the other lot (who always split the vote) think they know better than their Sovereign masters and mistresses – the people of Great Britain and her territories.

Legislators have procrastinated in every way in order to either get the best possible outcome, which would be in the interest of their puppet masters, or reverse the people's decision entirely.

The leave voters might have won the day by just a small 52% victory, but it was still a majority in what was a fair and democratic process. Yet since the decision to leave was announced we have been bored to death with the antics of those who are about to lose their cushy jobs in government, banking and commerce.

In this little book I investigate the pros and cons of our membership of the European Union. I admit from the start that I did not have all of the information when I was invited to cast my vote and it was a chance reading that caused me to vote to leave.

Since the result of the vote has been ignored I have made it my business to learn all I can about the European Union. How it functions, who gains the most and who gains the least (there do not appear to be any outright losers) and how it has effected our life, good or bad in the United Kingdom; and what I have discovered has made me even more sure of my decision to vote to leave.

If, in keeping with the rest of the country, my gentle reader felt that you were having to take a view based on limited knowledge I feel that the contents of this little book will introduce you to great food for thought and if you voted to leave you will be even more sure of your stance as in deed I was.

If, on the other hand, you voted to remain I think what you are about to read will either change your mind over your decision completely or it will cause you to have some reservations; at any rate I feel sure it will introduce you to issues of which, you might not have been aware.

December 2020

Ted Moss

CONTENTS

ACKNOWLEDGEMENTS

My felicitations and my thanks to that great man, Oscar Fingal O'Flahertie Wills Wilde (16 October 1854 – 30 November 1900)

Unless mentioned otherwise, images and illustrations in this book are due to the good offices of https://pixabay.com an international free-to-use website for sharing photos, illustrations, and graphics.

I have found Wikipedia to be an excellent source of reference materials for which I extend my gratitude.

ALSO BY THIS AUTHOR

HOME & HELP eBOOK SERIES

Win Job Interviews

Equaliser

Little Black Book of Debt

Essential Consumer Handbook

Conveyancing Without a Solicitor

The Art of House Agency

Plumbing Jobs Around The House

Blueprint for Success

Prosper Writing CVs

Compendium of Careers

Meaning of Dreams

Arts, Craft, Hobbies & Collectibles

How Many Beans Make Five?

To access the above free ebooks

send a blank email to:

itedmoss@gmail.com

putting Home and Help in the subject line.

STAND ALONE NOVELS

The Ten Percent Man
ISBN: 978-1-4452-7322-8 Paperback
ISBN: 978-1-4457-1566-7 Hardback

The Laird Of Glendawn
ISBN 978-1-4092-0586-9 Paperback
ISBN 978-1-4457-1580-3 Hardback

UNPALATABLE TRUTHS

Are Gods A Fabrication Of The Mind Of Man?
ISBN 978-1-7166-4600-3 Paperback

Homelessness Is Escalating Year After Year – Why?
ISBN 978-1-7165-8872-3 Paperback

The Festive Season Naughty Or Nice?
ISBN 978-1-7164-3513-3 Paperback

The European Union
Should We Stay Or Should We Go?
ISBN 978-1-716-39515-4 Paperback

FUTURE TITLES IN THE UNPALATABLE TRUTH SERIES ARE PLANNED

THE €UROP€AN UNION! SHOULD W€ STAY OR SHOULD W€ GO?

Did Vested Interests Blur The Issues, But Did The People Still Decide Wisely?

"I HAVE A CUNNING PLAN"

NOW, WHO DO WE ASSOCIATE WITH THAT STATEMENT? WHY! YES, OF COURSE, BALDRICK FROM BLACK ADDER!

I suggested above that David Cameron might have jumped ship from the Conservative Party due to the result of the United Kingdom European Union membership referendum when he was the Prime Minister. If so, then that begs the question, did Cameron know there would be a right ol' cross-party argy-bargy if 'Leave' was the result of the EU membership referendum? And was a gullible woman allowed to win the nomination of the next person to lead the Conservative party, because unlike everybody else, she was unable to see the train coming down the track that would cause her so much misery, eventually derailing her premiership? Michael Gove had a narrow escape, apparently due more to his friends and good luck than to any intellectual reading of the situation – I recall something about him being advised to stand down for the sake of his political career.

Additionally, it seemed to be rather suspect that the man who always 'Would be King', that is prime minister, Boris Johnson, backed out of the race. Was Theresa May the fall guy? Or should that be was Theresa may the fall gal? I don't know the correct phrase to use, but here is a picture of the lady

TRESemmé
USED BY PROFESSIONALS ®

No! That's the wrong Theresa May.

Oh now, that's better. Whether or not she recognised it, within days of taking up her new role as Prime Minister she found herself in the *role* of the rope in a political game of Tug-o'-War.

Although she was a Conservative, it is difficult not to feel sorry for the silly woman as in landing the job of the boss of the UK she became the butt of many jokes, one of which was: *"she has a cunning plan"*. If she *had* taken a leaf out of Baldrick's book and had cunningly planned to steer a true course to take the UK to a speedy, successful exit from the EU, it was not clear; what was clear, however, was that she was never in the driving seat.

From what we witnessed over the years she was in office it would appear that Theresa May was being bullied by servants of a cabal of elitist. People who have a lot to lose and business interests that will not come to fruition if Britain was to leave the EU at all! And still stand to bear loses if we leave without a deal that suits them so between them they have hatched their own cunning plan.

Unlike Baldrick's harmless cunning plans, however, which always go awry, if the elitists are allowed to implement their cunning plan it will drop a bombshell on the people of Great Britain that we will all be smarting from for years to come.

Using timid Theresa May (the washed-out one not the hair wash one) these people with business agendas began their plan to sow the seeds of doubt in the minds of the electorate.

By purposely spreading malicious rumours devised to scare people into being of the opinion that leaving the European Union will be the equivalent of Armageddon, they caused many people to re-consider whether the decision to leave the EU was the right one and even causing some leave voters to completely doubt their decision.

Personally I feel (as the manipulating of minds is on going) this to be a criminal act – as like it or not – the result of the vote to leave the EU was democratically arrived at and should be left at that. Nevertheless, the pressure has been so successful that it has seen a politician, who really should have known better, succumb and another, more savvy politician, use it to his advantage.

As we know Theresa May reigned from 2016 to 2019. She has gone and now we really do have 'The Man Who Would be King,' we have Boris Johnson as Prime Minister and whereas Theresa May had shown herself to be ineffectual, Boris has shown himself to be quite tricky and a teller of *porkies,* which he would appear to have done to win the last election in order to continue the elitist's interests.

Boris Johnson won the general election of 2019 and his theme throughout appeared to be one of observing and supporting the people's decision and getting us out of the EU as soon as possible (this was the lie and although I say it myself, it was a clever piece of sleight-of-hand). The reason I say that is since then Johnson has been recorded as saying that he is in favour of remaining,

From this revelation we must deduce that Johnson will not be going all out to get us free of the EU without kowtowing to the EU suits to reach the deal that the elitists – his masters – want.

On the other hand, perhaps we would also be correct in deducing, if his masters requirements are not met, he might sabotage the whole democratically arrived at vote to leave the EU; even pushing through a second ballet after allowing the elitists more time to indoctrinate the electorate with its spin (which is governmentese for untruths, fibs, porkies or downright lies). And right out of the blue, Johnson's plans were given a boost from a completely unexpected source.

As if by osmosis the then leader of the opposition Labour party Jeremy Corbyn neatly assisted Boris's plans; although I am sure Jeremy did it unwittingly. Corbyn, probably still looking around for a razor, foolishly stated that he would support a second referendum, and as such walked straight into Boris's trap.

Did the people vote for a Conservative win in the 2019 general election because Johnson appeared to be promising to honour the people's decision to leave the EU? We will probably never know, although, in hindsight, a promise to leave would seem to have been the safe horse to back and it was the horse that Corbyn should have been riding.

Due to his thoughtless and very wrong statement, Corbyn probably lost the 2019 general election for the Labour party, together with his job as leader of the Labour party and because of that, we the people have lost any chance we might have had to leave the EU on our terms, meaning *No Deal*!

If Johnson and the cabal have their way we will not be getting out Scot-free, but will remain connected to the EU with all of the pain but none of the pleasure. If that was to happen does it mean the centuries of British constitutional reform count for nothing and have gone to the wall?

Does it mean that our darling parliamentarians on orders from their puppet masters have set a precedent for future governments to take heed of? Does it mean that if the result of the next general election does not meet with the requirements of the cabal, it will be able to force a review and even overturn the vote? Does it mean that powerful groups will in future be allowed to procrastinate, delaying the will of the people?

No, it certainly does not and it is dangerous to even think like that and it is a good reason why we must ensure that the returned result of the democratic referendum on Britain leaving the European Union is carried through without further hindrance and compromise.

THE EUROPEAN UNION

Although the following is something of a simplified overview of the Common Market (European Economic Community, originally the Treaty of Rome) I feel it is a fair assessment.

The European Economic Community (EEC) was formed in 1958 after World War 2, to provide an economic, reciprocal trading agreement between countries. The original six participating countries were Belgium, Germany, France, Italy, Luxembourg and the Netherlands. The union of countries enabled them to trade unhampered, thereby being more likely to avoid conflict and future war.

Since its inception the EU powers began to grow and it now makes policy on climate, environment, health, justice and migration issues. The EU has also grown physically and the original foundation member states have increased to 27, 28 if we count the UK.

The abolition of border controls between EU countries means people travel freely throughout most of the continent. It has become much easier both to live, and work abroad in Europe as all EU citizens have the right and freedom to choose in which EU country they want to study, work or retire. Countries in the EU must treat all citizens with respect the way they would their own people especially in areas of employment and rights to benefits.

Now, on the face of it, all of the above sounds good and would make sense, especially the part about keeping conflicts at bay and preventing war and the EU claims to have delivered over half a century of peace, stability and prosperity and helped raise living standards throughout; however, I find it difficult to accept that claim in its entirety.

Half a century of peace might be acceptable for the majority of member states not fighting each other; however, I would have thought that Ireland would take issue with the time scale.

The Good Friday Agreement, 1998, is generally accepted as the withdrawal of UK troops from Ireland and an end to the troubles. Yet the United Kingdom and the Republic of Ireland were still fighting even though both countries had joined the European Union in 1973. To underline that point: Britain and The Republic of Ireland were fighting for 25 years during their membership of the EU.

I have not set out to bash the European Union, the concept of which must be seen as nothing short of commendable. It is the unchecked Bureaucratic power mongers and the self-serving Eurocrats that I have the problems with, Particularly when these people's decision making powers cause the people of the UK to suffer.

We are an Island, it has always been our strength. We are a Sovereign People living in a Sovereign land. We have our own currency. We have are own military. We have that piece of water surrounding us like a medieval moat (the sooner we collapse that tunnel the better).

We were a manufacturing nation and can be again. We do not need to belong to a club, especially a club that leeches off us! We are a Global Power, and although we might call on the USA for support, on our own we are still formidable.

In this little book we shall be looking at the reasons for staying in the European Union or leaving it as the British people voted.

INTRODUCTION

Before I begin writing seriously on this subject, I need to say at the outset that I am not an expert on the United Kingdom's relationship with the European Union.

What you are about to read is the information, which I have managed to figure out after months of research, observation and thought. I feel the issues facing us are rather quite simple and are:

- *Developing profitable markets via free trade with over 90% of countries outside of the European Union.*
- *Leaving the EU without paying any fees whatsoever.*
- *The reciprocal acquisition of foreign property and liabilities.*
- *The protection and rights of migrant people.*

I am quite sure I have seen through the many 'smoke screens' that serve to obscure the issues and make an apparently simple procedure unnecessarily difficult and complex; all of which I feel are no accidents, but have been purposely created by devious minds to mislead the people.

The subject of deception brings to mind a most famous saying that is attributed to Abraham Lincoln and throughout the whole of my research and deliberations I have borne in mind the words of this most popular American President who said:

In the referendum of 2016 the public as a whole knew very little of the issues involved and, in trying to convince us to vote a certain way, the interested parties did not help matters. The arguments around stay or go were many and as the interested parties put their logical sounding arguments so forcefully and convincingly it was difficult for many people to know which way they should vote in the best interests of the people and the country.

I do not know why others chose to vote the way they did, I can only speak for myself, I was a leave voter and I will tell you now that I was not persuaded by any politician. Not by thinking that Farage's or Johnson's arguments were stronger for us to leave the EU, or thinking that Cameron's arguments for us to stay in the EU were weaker.

I voted leave after looking into as much of the arguments as I could understand at the time and I discovered something that worried me greatly.

I read about a secret cabal comprising of American, English and European Union member state business people who, if the voters opted to stay in the European Union, had contrived a plan to take into full private ownership the United Kingdom's most precious possession.

An alliance had been formed to first weaken the NHS by hyping up the price of drugs and then pouncing on the National Health Service when it was at its weakest and stealing it right from under us, for a pittance.

My gentle reader will no doubt be aware now of the Transatlantic Trade and Investment Partnership, or TTIP. It is still very much alive and vying for us to remain in the EU. And it was at the heart of Andrew Lansley's 'Liberating the NHS', white paper.

I think of all that needs protecting in the UK, the top of the list must surely be the National Health Service and that was the only reason I voted to leave in 2016. However, since then my resolve to leave has been strengthened greatly after reading about the misdirections taking place.

We will take a look at those misdirection strategies in detail presently. However before we do I should like to mention a piece of Government skulduggery, which once again is aimed at the NHS.

Although implementation of the policy would not be as a direct consequence of the (Remain, or Leave on elitist's terms) debate. Yet, it is likely to be an indirect result that appears to have been engineered to weaken the National Heath Service and in that respect it deserves my bringing it to the attention of my gentle reader.

For a thorough explanation one is advised to explore the Transformation and Sustainability Plans, however, the main points of the plans are as follows:

KEY THEMES OF THE SUSTAINABILITY AND TRANSFORMATION PLANS (STPs)

- More closely integrate heath and social care services, encourage GPs to work together at greater scale and deliver a wider range of services in the community

- Promote healthy lifestyles, support people to manage their own health, address wider social factors that influence good health.

- Improve care in specific areas (such as mental health) depending on local health needs, workforce and quality issues and national requirements

- Centralise some acute services on fewer sites, reconfigure how specialised services are delivered and in some cases reduce hospital capacity

- Develop integrated approaches to commissioning new contracting models and payment systems focused on care outcomes and closer NHS and social care collaboration

- Reduce variation in clinical practice and deliver efficiencies in non-clinical services such as procurement and estates

- Develop IT and digital services, such as electronic health records and health apps' and make changes to the NHS estates, such as disposing of unused assets and developing new facilities

- Improve staff recruitment, reduce agency costs and develop new skills and roles such as health coaching and care co-ordination

With some effort, it was possible to understand what the various clauses were saying. But should not the simplest of minds easily comprehend a document advising of situations that will apply to us all? This might be seen as an example of what George Orwell would call Newspeak.

Newspeak or Doublespeak is the sort of language used by politicians to disguise or completely evade the truth. It is an interesting subject and one in which I spend more time studying in another volume in the Unpalatable Truth series of social comment books. Please see, Homelessness Is Escalating Year After Year Why? ISBN 978-1-7165-8872-3 Paperback. In a little while we shall revisit the concept of Newspeak.

SCARE TACTICS

Having tried unsuccessfully to secure a leaving agreement that suited them, those with the most to lose have generated scare tactics to convince the public into believing that leaving without an agreement will see food prices rise and people will be put out of work and we will all end up worse off.

And just look at the calibre of people who are spreading these rumours: *"A hard Brexit will lead to 22% EU food tariffs."* Nick Clegg warns us in the Financial Times, October 2016. Ask yourself, how can this be if we are not dealing with the EU?

What the hell does *Brexit* mean and where did that term come from anyhow? It sounds like something to describe the first meal of the day. "Come on now kids eat up your Brexit cereal and you'll grow big and strong".

Alright, I know, it's not describing the breakfast cereal, but it is describing something. I think it is about getting out of something; the exit bit on the end sort of gives that away (nothing much gets past me), but what does the BR or Br stand for and why did that low-life call it hard? Are we getting out of British Rail? That would make sense because their rolling stock is solid because it is made of steel, which is hard! Okay, I know, I'm joking, I'm having a laugh at the messengers of doom, I think we are all entitled to laugh at them because they have been laughing at us throughout this whole EU referendum fiasco.

Before I went on an expedition to find who coined the term I thought I would discover it to have been invented by some newspaper editor as catchy names and phrases are so beloved of newspaper editors. They really do like to flex that part of their brains, which is devoted to inventing catchy labels to put on things and even on people. But why *Brexit*? I mean Br standing for Britain is not representative of the whole word, 'Bexit' would make more sense. There are other catchy labels that would make more sense as well, something like...

TUKout (The United Kingdom out), or...
GBout, we might even have…
EUgo, pronounced (yougo), or perhaps…
Bexodus, or even…
VamoosEU...

I tried to fit in a catchy phase containing Treaty of Rome and the Common Market, but I think we will leave it at those mentioned. The whole point is, why do we need a catchy phrase at all? The people in 2016 voted 'OUT!' That should have been enough and Britain's membership of the Common Market should be a long forgotten unhappy memory today. Incidentally it seems that somebody by the name of Peter Wilding came up with the term *Brexit*, he was head of a Tory think tank on remaining in the EU, fancy!

Clegg's mention of a *hard Brexit* is yet another attempt to muddy the waters and deceive us; there is no such thing. It is a term invented by those who stand to lose if we leave the EU without a deal or without a deal that suits them. And how could we ever believe anything that came out of the mouth of Nick Clegg, the turncoat who persuaded Labour voters to trust him and then took those Labour votes and gave them to the Tories to form a coalition with Cameron to stand against Labour?

If my gentle reader voted for him, don't feel bad we all make mistakes, it's not the end of the World. Politicians are good at *misdirection*, it's their stock-in-trade. They will lie to your face and when caught out in a lie or *spin* as they call it, they come out with things like: *"I'm sorry if you thought I was not being transparent"*, or some such rubbish. As we have learned this is what George Orwell called *Newspeak.*

As mentioned earlier it is a term for how politicians are coached in answering uncomfortable questions often put to them by the media. We need to learn from the way politicians talk in order that we might easily recognise it in the future. Therefore, at the end of this book, my gentle reader will find many examples of Newspeak.

Do not ever believe, out of hand, a word that a politician says, as they all have hidden agendas, check it out for yourself. I do not care who they are Tories, Labour, Liberal and the rest. Ask yourself this question: Why did these people go into politics? I'll tell you now it was not for you or the people in the next town so it must have been for themselves. And who can really blame them though when by all accounts they all retire on very handsome pensions.

I don't blame them as long as they use their exalted positions to help the people who need and deserve help, but if they seem not to be doing that, regardless of my loyalties, I have to question their motives. Take for example Jeremy Corbyn. We have mentioned how he was sucker punched by Johnson.

He has said he would back a second referendum, really? This apparent man of the people is quite content to go against a major decision, democratically arrived at by a majority of the Sovereign people of the United Kingdom; in my view that is unforgivable.

He adds to his willingness to sell 'the people' down the river by standing against a No-Deal withdrawal from the European Union. For some reason this man of the people wants to allow Brussels to continue to control us – why? There is no reason why we cannot just walk away from the club.

The Government's own lawyers have told them that we can freely walk away from our membership of the European Union without having to pay it a red cent. Meaning no mula, zilch, nothing, not a dicky bird, not a sausage, nothing, zero, nowt. Is my gentle reader beginning to get the picture?

MORE SCARE TACTICS

One of the elitist, David Tyler, boss of the Sainsbury Supermarket Group warned: *"A no deal Brexit would raise the cost of shopping"* The Sunday Times, October 2017. Pretty much the same as the turncoat, Clegg said. Might they be sleeping together? Just a thought!

And the bosses of all the supermarket chains have pretty much said something along the same lines. There is absolutely no basis for making such statements, they are untruthful, unhelpful and tend to cause confusion and trouble, which it would seem is why they are made.

Besides the scaremongering that leaving the EU will see food prices increase the harbingers of doom wish us all to believe we will be put out of work as factory after factory closes down as an inevitable consequence directly attributable to leaving the European Union without a deal that suits the suits (pardon the pun).

Once again, there is no substance whatsoever to these claims, they are desperate bids to get the people to accept a deal in favour of the elitists or agree to a new referendum and to vote to stay in the EU.

This sort of trouble making really angers me as we are being spoken to as if we are stupid. We need to understand that capitalists will close factories all the time and they don't appear to give a damn for the workers, Dyson for example.

James Dyson shifted production to Singapore in 2002 putting nearly 1000 people out of work in and around Malmesbury, Wiltshire. The move caused conflict with trades unions and controversy in the town and rumour emerged suggesting the move was all about cheap labour. However, I must emphasise that it was rumour; still taking similar example into consideration my gentle reader will have one's own thoughts.

TO UNDERLINE THE ABOVE STATEMENT

We should never forget that we have a skilled workforce capable of making Buses, Trains, Ships (and vacuum cleaners for that matter) in the UK, yet who considered the plight of the UK workforce when the contracts to build buses went to Belgium?

In a letter to the Belfast Telegraph Dr William Wright, co-founder of the global bus builder Wrightbus, has asked Regional Development Minister Michelle McIlveen to intervene after a Belgian firm won a £19m contract to build thirty new buses for Belfast.

The contract to build trains for the UK went to Spain: Unions say a decision to give a Spanish company a £490m contract to build trains for the UK railways is a 'kick in the teeth' for the British worker.

Keeping thousands of people on the dole, the contracts for building ships went to *other EU countries* rather than here in the UK where we have a glorious history of ship building and a wealth of experience necessary to build them.

We have British Shipbuilders on the river Clyde, Harland and Wolff in Belfast (which we allow to be owned by Fred Olsen Engineering of Norway) and Cammell Lairds on the river Mersey for starters.

These ship yards stand idle with rusting cranes and other ship building machinery, having been left to the elements, lying derelict for years while contracts for work go abroad to other European Union countries – how is that fair?

"THE UK Government has come under fire for handing out multi-million pound contracts to European Union countries instead of British ones. The steel for the £8 billion project for eight new Navy ships – the Type26 frigate – would come from Sweden.

"And a fresh blow was delivered to UK industries when shipbuilders BAE systems released procurement contracts, totalling £64 million, listing six European countries who have snatched work from the UK."

Sunday Express, Thursday, August 10th 2017.

A rumour suggested that the steel for the Type26 frigate was being bought in Sweden, which seems to be correct, however, that the steel was being sent to a German shipyard to construct the ships, was without confirmation.

Today the exact position is unclear as it seems Clydebank ship yards are building the new Type26 frigate. It has been difficult to see when the 'U' turn was made, but it would appear that the SNP's MP for West Dunbartonshire, Martin Docherty-Hughes had pushed the issue in the house causing the then Defence Minister Harriet Baldwin to revisit the decision to award the contract out of the UK.

Just to underline a point that might not have been immediately noticed in all the information that my gentle reader has been asked to absorb. The £8 billion contract to buy steel from Sweden and the attempt to hand over a £64 million contract to, […] the five European Union countries who have snatched work from the UK [...] were implemented 14 months after the Sovereign British people had given an order to the Government that said: "Get Us The Hell Out Of Dodge!"

WHILE WE ARE ALL AT SEA WE NEED TO REMEMBER THE COMMON FISHING POLICY

The Common Fishing Policy (1970) (CFP) signalled the huge decline of our fish stocks, deterioration of the environment, wasteful discarding of fish, and the destruction of Britain's fishing industry, dependent industries and communities. British waters account for *60% of the EU's fishing grounds* and a painful reminder is: that the *CFP did not exist* until Britain joined the EU. They *need us more* than we will ever need them.

[…] In leaving the EU without a deal the UK will regain control of lost fishing rights around our coast, where over *50% of the catch* is currently being taken by EU boats. Since the early 70's the (CFP) is estimated to have taken around 10,000 jobs (more dwindling each year) away from British fishermen and dependent communities and not forgetting the value of those extra lost catches, estimated to be worth over £2 Billion a year [...] 'The Commentator 2019'.

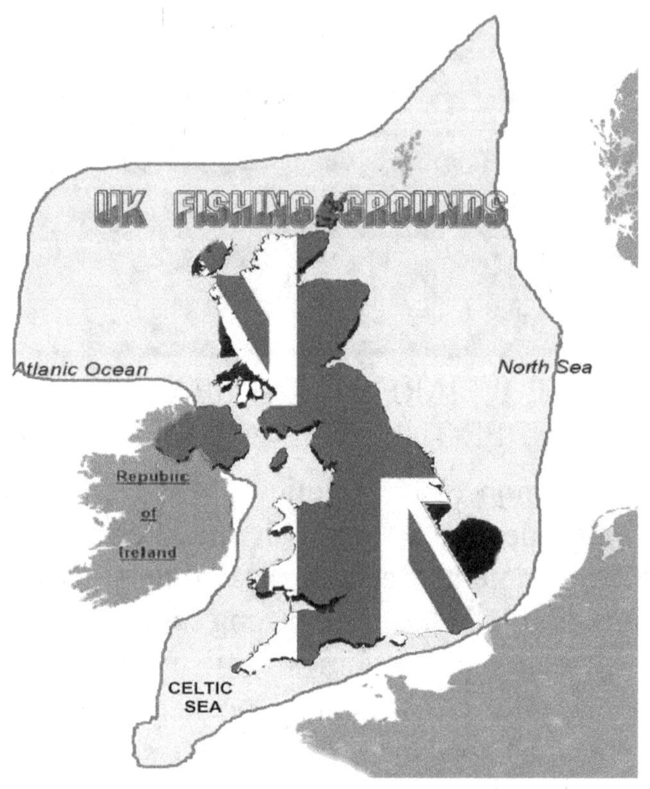

Furthermore, this is not something new. Our politicians have been selling us down the river for years, so much so that the rest of the world has begun to call us *Treasure Island*. They see the United Kingdom as somewhere one can pick up a car company for a snip; or… "alwight Governor? 'onest Johns the name, an' UK flog-offs is the game; if you're in the market for a power company Guv, I can let you 'ave this one cheap, it's a real kosher deal my son".

"Roll-up, roll-up, come and see my wares; I've got Car companies, Gas companies, Electric companies, Water companies and if I 'avent got what yea want now my son, I'll 'ave it for yea, by the end of the day, stand on me Guv, now would I lie to you?"

Since the Thatcher and her mate Milton Friedman made an appearance that is how it has been. It's like a market stall on the Portobello road, everything in Britain that is not welded, nailed or screwed to the ground is up for grabs if you have the mula. Treasure Island? More like Father Christmas's Grotto.

If my gentle reader thinks I am joking, I wish I was. The way I spoke might have been humorous, but the content was anything but. As far back as 2014 the

Independent Newspaper reported that foreign governments are making hundreds of millions of pounds a year running British public services, which is benefiting overseas, rather than UK, taxpayers.

"Swathes of Britain's energy, transport and utility networks are run by companies owned by other European governments, for example France owns an electricity company and Germany owns a water company, meaning foreign exchequers reap the dividends while UK customers struggle with increasing fares and bills." The Independent Thursday 20 November 2014.

The North Sea gas fields were sold to Oil and Gas interests in North America. Although not the EU, it reinforces the point that our governments have sold off anything and everything that have provided jobs to the UK workforce and lost complete control over any ability to provide work for our people.

THE EUROPEAN UNION NEED US MORE THAN WE NEED IT

And That Goes For The Movers And Shakers In The United Kingdom

It is the Capitalists themselves who are worried about this exit debacle and they are worried because it is them who will lose and we should not be concerned about them one iota. In the words of that wonderful thinker Michael Foot:

[...] If you ask me about those insoluble economic problems that may arise if the top is deprived of their initiative, I would answer 'To hell with them.' The top is greedy and mean and will always find a way to take care of themselves. They always do [...]

I applaud Michael Foot and my answer to factories closing is the same as he would have said: We would open them immediately. They are in the UK, the UK provided the land for them, the UK financed the buildings, the UK part financed, or in some cases fully financed the machinery and the UK gave the operators special rent and rate concessions.

If a member country of the EU has a factory in the UK and closes it after a no-deal withdrawal from the European Union, is there any reason why Britain could not take it over and continue to make the fridges, washing machines cars, motorcycles etc?

We used to do it. Who can remember the Hillman Minx, the Morris Minor, the Austin Cambridge, the Standard Vanguard? Or the Norton SS, the Triumph Bonneville, the Douglas Dragonfly, the Ariel Square Four?

Our wonderful workforce built them and sold them in the sixties and we would do it again and without charging tariffs to our new customers all around the world.

Of course they would need to be redesigned and modernised, but we have the clever young people with the brilliant brains in our country to do it.

We would have the more than 90% of the world outside of the EU in which to sell our goods and as we would not be levying tariffs, but would be dealing in free trade as so many other countries in the world do, would we not attract more business than the EU ever did?

Ah! Of course, it makes perfect sense when you think about it. If we leave without strings tying us to the EU, we could beat it on world trade and probably bankrupt it and then other countries in the EU will leave and the non-elected Eurocrat's gravy train will come off the rails to a crashing halt! We can see the cracks are starting to show now.

SHOULD WE REMAIN OR LEAVE?

Should we stay as a member of the European Union or should we go it on our own – like we always did?

Below follows brief overviews of the arguments of the REMAIN and the LEAVE campaigners.

1. PRICES. Issues guaranteed to generate fear and confusion.

REMAIN ARGUE:

Food prices will rise if we leave the EU without a deal. Tariffs on clothes will rise by at least 10 percent, by 37 percent on meat and 45 percent on dairy products. From the 30th March 2019, the UK will no longer be covered by international trade agreements, so in a no-deal exit, prices would be affected by a new average tariff of 27% on food and drink from the EU meaning imported goods will be subject to higher tariffs and potential customs barriers, meaning higher prices.

LEAVE ARGUE:

The remain campaigners are bombarding us with lie after lie. Lies such as those concerning a Custom's Union and the scaremongering that prices will go sky-high if we leave. When the reality is prices will decease as we will not be locked into tariffs and can deal with whoever we want in this great big world. Once freed from the protectionist rules, we can trade with over 90% of the world that are not part of the EU.

Speaking about tariffs all the scaremongers would

The free trade no-deal option won't work because this would leave government with a hole in its finances where the tariffs income used to be so the losses from cancelled tariffs would be outweighed by the benefits of attracting new international business.

Power is in the hands of the EU negotiators, who can stop the UK from leaving. They say: we must pay £39 billion to stay in the customs union and agree EU's terms over Ireland etc.

have us think that the £93 Billion collected by the UK would be lost to our economy if we leave, but this is nonsense. The revenues generated from the tariffs charged on goods entering all EU countries from non-EU countries, including the UK, goes to Brussels; the member states do not get it.

With regard to the idea about the UK not being able to avoid the payment of £39 billion to the EU is also nonsense. Government lawyers have said there is no obligation to pay and the UK could quit the EU without paying a cent.

2. MEMBERSHIP FEE. What it costs us to be in the club.

REMAIN ARGUE:

In 2016, Britain paid in £13.1bn, but it also received £4.5bn worth of spending. So the UK's net contribution was £8.6bn.

Outside the EU, British businesses would suffer, factories would close and people would be put out of work because the UK would lose trade and reduce its power to negotiate deals with the rest of the world which would cost more than the £8.6bn.

LEAVE ARGUE:

To put that another way: In 2016, The UK poured £8.6bn down the drain! The Remainers appear to say it's alright to pour £8.6bn down the drain, as the loss would be over compensated by the fact that if we leave the rest of the world would not trade with us or would impose such severe tariffs as to make trade impossible.

When free of protectionist constraints of the EU, of course, the UK would strike trade agreements with countries outside of the EU. And quite the opposite of a barren wasteland, Britain would bloom by replicating free trade agreements with the likes of: Australia, New Zealand, Israel, Canada, Singapore and Switzerland.

3. INVESTMENT. This promises to chew away at Bankers' powers.

REMAIN ARGUE:

LEAVE ARGUE:

The UK's standing as one of the world's financial hubs would be severely reduced if it ceased to be the vehicle into the EU for the likes of US banks; and UK financial institutions would encounter difficulties doing business across the continent.

Banks, Insurance companies and Assurance companies have begun to establish new bases in the EU and are starting to move staff.

People have said to me that particular remain argument opposite is aimed at scaring people into thinking we will lose our money and have no banking facilities in this country if we leave without a deal.

That is total nonsense and once free of EU rules and regulations, the UK could reinvent itself as a supercharged, Singapore-style Economic Power-House.

4. *SOVEREIGNTY.*

REMAIN ARGUE:	**LEAVE ARGUE:**

EU membership involves trading sovereignty for influence enabling Britain with a seat at the negotiating table, amplifying our voice on the world stage.

Quitting the EU will not enhance our national sovereignty, it would weaken it by removing our power to influence events in an interdependent world.

We need to remember that we are a Sovereign people. And that we are an island and that has always been our strength. Germany could not just walk into Britain as it walked into France and Poland.

When the UK was looking to join the EU it was suggested that Edward Heath's Government would be giving up the Sovereignty of these lands and as such he was guilty of committing treason according to the Treason, Felony Act of 1848.

An argument that says we should never have joined the EU, therefore we are right to leave.

5. IMMIGRATION.

REMAIN ARGUE:	**LEAVE ARGUE:**

While the pace of immigration had led to some difficulties with housing and service provision, the net effect had been positive overall.

The free movement of people throughout the EU had opened job opportunities for British workers seeking to work in Europe.

Under EU law, anyone from a member state can live in the UK. This has resulted in a huge increase in immigration, which services are struggling to cope with.

942,000 eastern Europeans entered the UK, along with 791,000 western Europeans and 2.93m workers from outside the EU in 2016. Source: Office for National Statistics 2016

The UK should take back control of borders, not necessarily to reduce immigration, but it should be up to the British Government to set the rules.

6. EMPLOYMENT.

REMAIN ARGUE:

Three million jobs would go if Britain left the EU.

"Limiting freedom of movement would deter the brightest and the best of the continent from coming to Britain and reduce the pool of candidates employers can choose from."
Professor Adrian Favell, London School of Economics.

LEAVE ARGUE:

Although around three million jobs are linked to trade with the EU they are not dependent on membership.

All those coming into Britain to work, especially the brightest and best, from anywhere would be welcomed with open arms, but only those who come to work, not for welfare.

A foreign worker's tax on employers, would ensure that and would also ensure that dishonest employers were not replacing British worker's jobs by taking advantage of foreigners to perform as cheap labour.

7. SECURITY.

<table>
<tr><td>REMAIN ARGUE:</td><td>LEAVE ARGUE:</td></tr>
</table>

REMAIN ARGUE:	LEAVE ARGUE:
[…] The UK benefited from being part of the EU, it is through the EU that information and criminal records are exchanged and how work on terrorism is progressed. The collective weight of the EU is required when dealing with the likes of Russian aggression [...] Defence Secretary Michael Fallon	The exchanging of critical information would continue unabated. The EU would not dare put lives at risk by refusing to cooperate, the UN would come down on them like a ton of bricks for just suggesting as much. Leaving will again enable us to control who enters and who stays outside of the United Kingdom.

TO PULL IT ALL TOGETHER

This book began by presenting an overview of the issues for leaving or remaining in the European union. It then examined each of the arguments in more detail. We will now pull all of the issues together

On the 22nd June 2016 the Sovereign people of the United Kingdom went to the polls to vote in the United Kingdom European Union membership referendum and by a 51.9% majority the people of Great Britain voted to leave the European Union.

Since that time a number of cross party elitists whose cushy positions, career ambitions, personal and business interests that, for the most part, exist outside of the United Kingdom have made a determined assault on that set-in-stone judgment made by the Sovereign people of the United Kingdom of Great Britain.

With the intention of negotiating terms suitable to themselves or overturning the whole democratically arrived at decision, these elitists, who care not one jot for the people of the countries concerned, have their own agendas and are proposing something preposterous.

They are proposing that Britain agrees to be bound by the terms of the EU, but have no say in the making of the rules or revising the rules or in the running of the EU whatsoever.

In other words, an independent state, Britain, is being asked to consider placing its people under foreign jurisdiction and foreign legislation; which in reality is something approaching being slaves to that foreign jurisdiction.

We are living in a modern democracy, yet we are standing back and watching while a hand full of people deny a majority their voice in deciding laws governing our country for who knows how long and paying £39 billion a year for the privilege.

It is accepted for one to disagree with a majority view and put up arguments to be used at the next election, but one must accept and respect the current majority election result. However, this hallowed anchor point of democracy is in danger of losing its grip because this withdrawal from the European Union debate is turning ever so nasty.

People are being assailed with fearful stories of food shortages and arguments predicting all manner of disasters with people dying due to the lack of medicines and hospitals. Extravagant campaigns designed to sabotage the will of the people have been allowed to run unchecked, exceeding political boundaries.

The European Union seems determined to hurt Britain for daring to leave the club. TRESemm'e (whoops! talk about give a dog a bad name), During her time in office, Theresa May apparently painted us into a corner with her belief that we must find a deal and as such there is only one deal on offer; which as stated earlier is: WE PAY BUT HAVE NO SAY.

Because the woman seemed not to understand or was scared of the power she held over Brussels, or was 'frit' as Dennis Skinner might have put it...

...the EU think it can ride rough-shod over the UK and, because of our inadequate representation, that is exactly what it is doing.

Not only should we be getting out as quickly as possible on our terms, we should never have got involved in the first place. To quote Tony Benn, speaking about the setup of the European Union when we entered:

"I am against the 'Treaty of Rome' which entrenches 'laissez faire' as its philosophy and chooses 'bureaucracy' as its administrative method." Or put bluntly: Survival of the fittest using any means, hidden within red tape (my words).

Freed from EU regulations, the United Kingdom would go back to doing business with the rest of the world, recognising WTO (World Trade Organisation) rules, as indeed we did before Heath sacrificed our Sovereignty to the European Union (which it seems was not only wrong, but an action of treason and we did not join and are not a member of the EU at all).

Working within the terms of the WTO the UK could refrain from imposing tariffs or taxes on produce from within the European Union (provided the EU agreed to do the same). Such mutual recognition of standards would free up border controls and solve the Customs Union issue.

If the EU agreed not to charge us tariffs we would agree not to charge it, consequently, it would be in the European Union's interest to accept this agreement as this reciprocation of considerations would maintain a free flow of goods both in and out of the United Kingdom and the EU, but this could never be if we allowed the EU to set the terms of a deal.

This is because the deal they would have us agree to, would bind us to the EU, have us abide by it's rulings and yet have no say whatsoever in the running of the club (oh, yes, we would still be expected to pay huge sums of money each year into the club as well). When we speak of a No Deal withdrawal from the European Union it means rejecting any deal the EU might wish to foist upon us and expect us to abided by.

Therefore, as far as the EU is concerned it would be a No Deal, because we would be leaving on our terms and, our terms are quite simple and are not open to negotiation.

THE UK'S NO DEAL NON NEGOTIABLE TERMS ON LEAVING THE EU

When Boris Johnson came into office, replacing Theresa May as Prime Minister in July 2019 he promised if the European Union do not accept a deal favourable to the UK by October 2019, he would take the United Kingdom out of the European Union without a deal, but did he mean it, or was it yet more smoke and mirrors?

We have seen that Johnson's personal allegiances are with the Remain camp. And we have witnessed the Remain group's endeavours, apparently frustrating his efforts to take us out of the EU at the stated time and Johnson appearing to be doing nothing about it. Has this all been part of a carefully contrived strategy that has resulted in extending the exit period until, January 2021 for whatever dastardly scheme he is planning?

Johnson has proved to be a slippery fish and I feel it is prudent to be suspicious, to say the very least, that his idea of a no deal will not be one that is in the interests of the people of the UK; speaking of fish, our fishing grounds must be protected. Having said that and there is no doubt that the protection of our fishing grounds it is a priority; however, the main consideration on leaving the European Union must be the people. Therefore, on leaving the European Union we must ensure that the interests and the welfare of all peoples is paramount.

(1) Persons from European Union countries residing and working in the United Kingdom and persons from European Union countries residing and running businesses in the United Kingdom will have the undisputed right to remain living and working and running businesses in the United Kingdom permanently and may apply for citizenship of the United Kingdom.

(2) Persons from the United Kingdom residing and working in European Union countries and persons from the United Kingdom running businesses in European Union countries will have the same undisputed right to remain living and working and running businesses in the European Union permanently and may apply for citizenship of the member country.

(3) Reciprocal agreement that tariffs will not be levied, ensuring an unhampered movement of goods both in and out of the United Kingdom and the European Union.

(4) No fishing boat from the European Union shall enter or fish in the United Kingdom's fishing grounds without a licence issued by the United Kingdom. Should a fishing boat from the European Union be found to be fishing in the United Kingdom's fishing grounds without a licence both the catch and the vessel will be permanently confiscated and the crew members accommodated until the country or countries concerned pay recompense to the United

Kingdom and make arrangements to have its people repatriated.

If Johnson's terms for a no deal are the same, then reluctantly I will be forced to conclude that for the first time in my life I will have agreed with a Tory; however I seriously doubt I will be breaking the habit of a lifetime.

It must be borne in mind at all times that the essence of free trade is to be free of ties to any organisation that might be holding back and retarding progress. Therefore, we must break free of the constricting ties to the European Union once and for all; to paraphrase Karl Marx:

We Have Nothing To Lose But The Shackles Imposed Upon Us By Our Membership Of The EU!

Finally, I would say that there are those on this planet who want more and more and they do not care who or what gets in their way as they will crush them underfoot in their drive to satisfy their greed.

Such people are represented by a number of the parliamentarians of the EU, from all countries, including the United Kingdom and their puppet masters who use the individuals as tools to satiate their greed, whilst hiding in the shadows. This book has been concerned with distancing ourselves from these people and the only way to do that is to get out of the EU without a deal, meaning a deal on our terms.

The above paragraph brings us to the end of our examination of the European Union. However, the book is not finished yet. I mentioned a little earlier the language of Newspeak so dear to politicians, well here is that list I promised you.

NEWSPEAK

There is no doubt that governments are devious animals, no more so than our own crowd of tricksters who are not afraid to use Newspeak to bamboozle us when it suits their purpose with phrases that at times beggar belief in their obvious attempts to misdirect, even resorting to making up words.

Most Members of Parliament and Ministers are not well equipped with the wit or intellect to create confusing phrases and sentences instantly when put on the spot.

Therefore, Newspeak tends to be the preserve of the Permanent Secretaries to Ministers and other permanent Government personnel who might speak personally to media or brief his or her Minister before that Minister is interviewed by a journalist.

I have collected a number of confusing 'Newspeak' phrases (together what explanations of what they actually mean), which I offer for your amusement and I dare say annoyance that we should be treated like imbeciles.

If it pleases my gentle reader, you might wish to copy and add to them in a journal or notebook. If nothing else it is a way of keeping the brain active and interested and at the same time having a little fun.

Text in Bold represents the question asked

IN UPPER CASE TEXT WE HAVE THE NEWSPEAK RESPONSE

Italics symbolises an explanations of what the respondent is actually thinking and means.

Slithering out of questions of overspending.

WE ARE HAVING AFFORDABILITY CHALLENGES.

Meaning: We've cocked up and wasted taxpayers' money.

Slithering out of questions of firing people.

WE ARE REDUCING TRANSACTIONAL ACTIVITY, MOVING FROM MANUAL FOCUS TO TECHNOLOGY DRIVEN PROCESSES.

Meaning: We are sacking people and replacing them with computers.

Slithering out of questions of covering lies.

PUTTING A SPIN ON THINGS.

Meaning: Barefaced lying through teeth.

Slithering out of questions for holding innocent people.

ADMINISTRATIVE DETENTION.

Meaning: Imprisonment without trial.

Slithering out of questions to explaining a role.

SPIN DOCTOR.

Meaning: Government paid liar.

Slithering out of questions to costs increasing

IT'S NORMAL FOR AN OVER-PROGRAMMING POSITION AT POINTS IN SPENDING CYCLE.

Meaning: The contractor undervalued the costs and we gave them more than double again of your Dosh!

(1) Slithering out of questions of deceit.

WE SEE THAT CHECKS AND BALANCES ARE IN PLACE TO ENSURE VIEWERS ARE PRESENTED WITH AN UNBIASED VIEW OF DOMESTIC AND WORLD EVENTS.

Meaning: We create good/bad news to hide our dirty tricks.

Slithering out of questions of over kill.

ACCEPTABLE COLLATERAL DAMAGE

Meaning: Deaths and injuries of the innocent in military operations that we don't give a damn about

(2) Slithering out of questions of deceit.

THE PUBLIC ARE DISCERNING AND WE ENSURE THAT VARIED TASTES IN ENTERTAINMENT ARE CATERED FOR.

Meaning: We pressurise the BBC and encourage other TV stations to put out lots of anaesthetising programmes such as sport and soaps to keep the plebs asleep while we rip them off.

Slithering out of questions of lying

THE RIGHT HONOURABLE GENTLEMAN REGRETS MISLEADING THE COMMITTEE.

Meaning: This dis-honourable conman told barefaced lies and he's sorry, only because he was caught

Slithering out of questions concerning lack of progress.

WE'RE WORKING IN BROAD SPECTRUM.

Meaning: We haven't got a clue!

(1) Slithering out of questions suggesting Nepotism.

WE ARE APPLYING PERFORMANCE MANAGEMENT RELATED MEASURES.

Meaning: We're looking after our mates

Slithering out of questions of inadequacy.

COST ESTIMATION AT LONG-TERM VOLATILITY CRYSTALLISED AT A FASTER RATE THAN EXPECTED.

Meaning: We gave the contract to one of our mates who undervalued the job and we lost a shed load of taxpayers' money subsidising the job

Slithering out of questions that try to hide cost.

IT'S IMPRUDENT TO MENTION NUMBERS IN THE PUBLIC DOMAIN, WHICH WILL INEVITABLY BE MISREPRESENTED.

Meaning: The costs will skyrocket.

Slithering out of questions of profits before care.

OUR DOCTORS AND NURSES ARE STRIVING TO IMPLEMENT A PATIENT CARE OUTCOME.

Meaning: We know patients are dying unnecessarily

(2) Slithering out of questions suggesting Nepotism.

WE OUTSOURCE STRATEGIC MANAGEMENT FUNCTIONS TO THE SPECIALISTS.

Meaning. We give the plumb contracts to our mates.

Slithering out of questions caught out in a lie.

IT IS REGRETTABLE YOU FEEL A LACK OF TRANSPARENCY WAS DEMONSTRATED.

Meaning: We know, you know we lied through our teeth

Slithering out of questions suggesting lying.

IT IS UNFORTUNATE THAT THE RIGHT HONOURABLE SPEAKER/PM/ FOREIGN SECRETARY/HOME SECRETARY/ CAPTAIN OF INDUSTRY/BANK OFFICIAL ETC, ERRONEOUSLY GAVE A MISLEADING ACCOUNT.

Meaning: S/he is a bare faced, corrupt and deceitful bastard who lied through his/her teeth and dropped us all in the smelly stuff!

Slithering out of questions of a mistaken project.

THE DECISION TO FUND X WAS AN EXPRESSION OF OVER EXUBERANCE AND THOSE ALIGNED MIGHT HAVE BETTER TAKEN ADVANTAGE OF THE COLLECTIVE INTELLECT.

Meaning: Each and every one of them is an idiot.

Slithering out of questions relating to under supporting the Armed Services.

WE ARE REVISING A CHALLENGING DEFENCE CAPABILITY STRATEGY CONCERNING OPERATIVES AND MATERIALS.

Meaning (1): Cuts in a navy that is short of sailors for crippled war ships that are limping around the World powered by auxiliary engines because some idiot in charge of spares had never thought to buy them, so we haven't got the parts to fix the main engines and new main engines are too expensive to buy and install.

Meaning (2): Cuts in the RAF that is short of aircraft because they were sold cheaply for scrap but, are now seen to be just what we need and are being sold back to us at a huge loss to the taxpayer.

Furthermore, the air force has jets that it can't refuel in mid-air because another idiot in the Ministry neglected to insist that the codes for the software be included in the price paid for the technology. So now we have to pay the Americans each time we refuel one of our own jets from a tanker in mid-air.

Meaning (3): Cuts in recruiting and equipment in an army that asks parents to nip down to the Army and Navy stores and buy your child some body armour.

Meaning (4): Unable to safely dispose of nuclear waste from 20 yet to be de-commissioned (laid up, and waiting to be dismantled and, still containing radioactive material, in some cases leaking) nuclear submarines, which are being stored at a profit to the private sector, and a loss to the taxpayer, of hundreds of millions of pounds a year. For years the MOD has been allowed to ignore the problem, which has been increasing and now represents an enormous threat to our continued existence. [...] Estimates suggest a programme to rid us of the nuclear submarine problem will cost an ongoing £7.5 billion pounds over 120 years. [...] Source: Private Eye, edition 1385, 2015 and edition 1494, 2019.

And of course always at the top of the Permanent Secretary's Hit Parade. So munch so that Ministers and MPs no longer have to be coached as it comes as second nature to them all. Here follows an example of how this one powerful ploy might be brought into play

Question: 'Perhaps, Minister you would like to tell the people of this country why it took thirty-minutes for ambulances/firefighters to arrive at the scene of the burning flats/theatre/stadium resulting in the deaths and injuries of over 500 people?'

WELL JOHN OF COURSE THAT IS WOEFULLY REGRETTABLE. YOU WILL, HOWEVER, I AM SURE, UNDERSTAND THAT I AM UNABLE TO COMMENT WHILE HIS HONOUR, JUDGE SIR ALGERNON MONCRIEFF AND HIS TEAM'S INVESTIGATIONS ARE ONGOING? HOWEVER, I CAN SAY THIS JOHN, LESSONS HAVE BEEN LEARNED.

Let's just dissect that VERBAL DIARRHOEA

John (pally with interviewer). You will understand (sympathise with my difficult position). Investigations are ongoing (always works a treat especially when a tile is thrown in). Finally, more familiarity and the one they always fall for (Lessons have been learned). Oh, that's OK then! All in all, the old tried and tested, slithering, get out of jail free card that never fails:

'LESSONS HAVE BEEN LEARNED'.

INDEX